SO-EAY-467

TABLE OF CONTENTS

We use both U.S. and metric units of measure in discussing our binational region. All currency figures are U.S. dollars, unless noted as Canadian (Can$). Because currency exchange rates fluctuate, equivalents are not given.

UNDOING CAMP CREEK

When fur trapper Peter Skene Ogden led a hunting party through the high desert of central Oregon in 1825, he came across a region of tall grasslands and lush marshes. "The Soil on this Fork [is] remarkably rich," Ogden observed in the first written description of the Crooked River basin, and "the Grass seven feet high." He found creek banks "well lined with willows." Abundant beaver along the Crooked River and one of its branches, Camp Creek, led the trapper to exult, "I doubt if we should find another equal to it in any part of this country."[1]

Fifty years after Ogden's expedition, a surveyor for the new state of Oregon found a comparably lush landscape along Camp Creek: abundant bunchgrasses in the uplands, "meadow" along the valley floor. Yet by 1905, the scene had changed beyond recognition. At that time, Israel Russell of the U.S. Geological Survey found not a meadow but a vertical-walled canyon 25 feet deep, with Camp Creek trickling across the rocky bottom.

What happened? In other watersheds, mining, logging, or water projects reshaped the land, but at Camp Creek, grazing did the damage. The U.S. government gave cattle and sheep herders free rein over the area, charged them nothing, and in no way restricted their use of the public estate. As Israel Russell surmised, "The change … probably coincides with the introduction of domestic animals in such numbers that the surface covering of bunch grass was largely destroyed, and in consequence the run-off from the hills accelerated."[2]

By and large, this hands-off, free-for-all approach to land management is a thing of the past, yet government support for destructive land use continues. Fees for the privilege of grazing livestock on publicly owned land, first charged in 1934, have remained low enough, and restrictions on grazing loose enough, that livestock continue to bleed the Camp Creek basin of its soil. Old maps still show "Severance Reservoir" on Camp Creek. Created in 1952 by a local rancher, the 65-foot-deep reservoir had disappeared by 1977, replaced by a new flat meadow atop a million tons of dam-trapped sediment. At present-day Camp Creek, the University of Colorado's Charles Wilkinson found "few beaver, no willows to speak of, and no 7-foot-tall grasses at all."

Ever since it was taken from the Ute-Aztekan Indians, most of the Camp Creek area has been owned by the American public; for most of this century, it has been managed by the U.S. Bureau of Land Management (BLM). Beginning in the 1960s, BLM fenced off a few stretches from cattle, and inside, the creek has begun the long process of restoring itself. In places, sediment captured by recovering vegetation has enabled the streambed and water table to climb about one-fourth the height back up to pretrench levels. But most of the creek and its uplands continue to be heavily grazed, and funding for even the simplest restoration projects may not survive the current climate of fiscal conservatism and antigovernment sentiment. Many area ranchers—who pay about one-fourth the going private rate to graze their cattle on someone else's land—resent the intrusion on their perceived "rights" to use the valley cheaply and without restrictions.[3]

subsidy *n.* a grant by a government to a private person
or company to assist an enterprise deemed advanta-
geous to the public

subsidize *v.* to aid or promote (as a private enterprise)
with public money

—Merriam Webster's Collegiate Dictionary

Many people in western North America consider the modern
West a product of free enterprise working its way across a
resource-rich landscape. But government largesse has been as central
to the West's economic development as has entrepreneurial spirit. Government subsidies have shaped the region's economic identity. They
have also shaped its environment: subsidies promoting resource use are
a major hidden force behind the ongoing degradation of natural
systems in the Pacific Northwest. Governments seldom write actual
checks to people for ripping out a stream or otherwise damaging the
land. But many policies have the same effect: they provide billions
of dollars in financial rewards each year for activities that harm the
Northwest environment.

To their recipients, subsidies can be substantial windfalls, in some
cases making the difference between profitability and bankruptcy. But
to most people, they are an abstraction, obscured by economic jargon
and budgetary politics. Most antienvironmental subsidies are not
direct cash grants, like a welfare check, but indirect handouts such as
tax breaks, the sale of natural resources below market prices, and
exemptions from environmental laws. Though they have tremendous
impacts on resource extraction, hydropower, transportation, and other
sectors of our economy, these subsidies are difficult to quantify. How
much must the government charge to capture fair market value when
it sells publicly owned timber? How much to at least avoid losing
money? The answers to questions like these depend on various economic
assumptions and accounting techniques, and they are debated endlessly.

Even to those who grant subsidies, their full scale remains unknown. U.S. congressional investigations into natural resource subsidies have failed to unravel the "dizzying array" of government payments. Subsidies are found in a wide range of legislation, often hidden deep in the text of complex laws. They are distributed by an equally wide range of government agencies, many of which maintain few records of the benefits they dispense. A 1994 congressional report on subsidies to natural resource industries concluded, "Frequently, the government has little or no information about the resources that it has given away."[4]

Though their economic value can be elusive, subsidies have real impacts. Camp Creek—like many places across the Northwest—bears witness to the radical changes that can be caused by something as abstract as a subsidy. The frontier-era government of the United States subsidized the use of Camp Creek's water, soil, and vegetation absolutely: it gave them away for nothing. In all but title, cattlemen were given the grasslands. Miners were given the earth. Those who came first were given rights to all the water they could use, forever.

The pregrazing Camp Creek was unusual in at least one respect: its tall grasses stood out in the arid, mostly short-grass steppe of the interior Northwest. But in the twentieth century, Camp Creek is just one degraded watershed among thousands, indicator of a pervasive problem in the Northwest and beyond. Policies that arose when natural resources and public funds were considered abundant continue to dominate our lands and politics long after the era of abundance has closed.

Government subsidies of the frontier era and today have ostensibly had admirable goals: to provide economic opportunities, encourage home ownership, or promote other public benefits. Indeed, subsidies are an appropriate form of public policy: government's role is to support the public interest in cases where the market economy fails to do so. But many subsidies have unforeseen and harmful effects on natural systems and public welfare. Many no longer serve their intended purposes (such as supporting family farmers); indeed, they often subvert their original aims. The objectives of others (such as encouraging settlement of the western frontier) are no longer relevant to society. Yet subsidies have taken on a life of their own, bolstered by laws, contracts, or simply the weight of tradition. Most impose sizeable burdens on government coffers in a time of widening deficits and demands for balanced budgets.

MANY SUBSIDIES HAVE UNFORESEEN AND HARMFUL EFFECTS ON NATURAL SYSTEMS AND PUBLIC WELFARE.

Then as now, the line between a subsidy and a failure to control harmful activities is blurred. Both impose the costs of private actions on others; the two often go hand in hand. In the case of Camp Creek, the government has directly subsidized the creek's undoing by charging little or nothing for its use. It has implicitly subsidized its destruction by making other people—salmon fishing communities downstream, people who used the Crooked River for drinking water, or future generations—suffer the costs of a ruined watershed, instead of preventing its ruin.

Though these policies may have made sense in the nineteenth century, they do not today. Yet many of them are still in effect. In legal scholar Charles Wilkinson's memorable phrase, they are the "lords of yesterday." Other subsidies have been introduced more recently, during the World Wars or other times of economic hardship. In most cases, modern government handouts are less than complete: rather than giving away natural resources, capital, or services, they offer these benefits at rates below those that private firms charge or below the government's own costs of administering the subsidized activity. When business costs are borne by the government or by the rest of society, business is being subsidized by others.[5]

This report focuses on a small fraction of government programs that directly or indirectly subsidize our economy, those that have major impacts on the environment of the Pacific Northwest—defined here as the watersheds of rivers that drain through North America's temperate rain forest zone. It is a region of some 14 million people and a $300 billion economy, stretching from Alaska's Prince William Sound to the California redwoods and from the Pacific Ocean to the continental divide (see map, inside front cover).

This report does not aim to cover every government subsidy that might lead to ecological harm. Instead it focuses on actions that lower the costs of logging, mining, farming, using electricity, and driving— all economic activities with heavy impacts in the Pacific Northwest.

For the purposes of this report, subsidies are government activities that

- provide capital, goods, or services below their cost to the government
- provide capital, goods, or services below their market price
- reduce tax burdens below those on similar activities.

Government also lowers the costs of environmentally destructive businesses by allowing them to force others to pay the "external" costs—such as inhaling carcinogens or never seeing a salmon jump upstream. But these costs, notoriously difficult (if not impossible) to quantify, are beyond the scope of this report.

IN THE ABSENCE OF SOUND LAWS AND REGULATIONS, ANY ECONOMY WILL CONSUME AND POLLUTE NATURAL SYSTEMS.

Antienvironment giveaways often benefit the Northwest's resource-intensive industries, but such subsidies are not limited to what U.S. Labor Secretary Robert Reich has termed "corporate welfare." To some degree, nearly all northwesterners are on the antienvironmental dole, benefiting, for example, from some of the cheapest electricity in the world. And all northwesterners pay the costs—both fiscal and ecological—of our governments' hazardous handouts.

Giveaways are by no means the only cause of environmental degradation. In the absence of sound laws and regulations, any economy, subsidized or not, will consume and pollute natural systems. Subsidies

to environmentally harmful activities defeat other government policies aimed at protecting the public interest and exacerbate our economy's
inherent tendency to grow at the expense of natural systems. Worse,
they do so at our expense. Reducing them will adjust the prices of
goods and services to reflect more closely their costs to society and the
natural world, and thereby begin to reveal the ecological wakes of our
economic decisions. This information will in turn help guide people
and businesses toward an economy and a way of life that can last.

TIMBER

S ince the first towering firs were felled and milled here in the 1850s, governments at all levels have greatly aided the Northwest timber industry's quest to turn the region's forests into wood and paper products. Some communities have enjoyed at least sporadic prosperity as a result, but through taxes and economic opportunities lost to rapid, environmentally unsound logging, others throughout the region and beyond have paid dearly for the industry's privileges. Modern logging has tremendous impacts on the region's forests, soils, and waters. Despite recent environmental restrictions, the scale of the industry remains enormous: loggers fell more old-growth forest annually in British Columbia, for example, than has ever been cut in a single year in all the national forests in the United States.[6]

The logic of the market has always favored the liquidation of natural capital; the illogic of skewed public policy has spurred it on. A variety of government supports artificially inflate pressures on forests by lowering timber costs, leaving taxpayers and ecosystems to pay the true costs.

British Columbia is a vast area—the size of Oregon, Washington, and California combined—half covered with trees. As in the rest of the Northwest, much of the land is publicly owned (see Table 1). In theory, public ownership means that much of the regional landscape should be managed in the public interest. In practice, it means that subsidies to industrial resource extraction operate on a massive scale.[7]

Most of British Columbia consists of "Crown lands" under the authority of the provincial Ministry of Forests, and timber companies have been granted the right to log many of these lands under "tree farm licenses" or other long-term agreements. One might expect an agency that sells off public assets to make money doing so, but the

Table 1. Pacific Northwest Land Ownership

Region	Total Land Area (million acres)	Public Land[a] (percent)	Private Land (percent)
British Columbia	234	94	6
Idaho	53	69	31
Oregon	62	50	50
Washington	43	36	64
Northwest California[b]	12	41	59
Southeast Alaska[c]	42	93	7
Western Montana[d]	16	56	44
Total	462[e]	77	23

[a] Tribal land is classified as public land in Canada and as private land in the United States.
[b] Del Norte, Humboldt, Mendocino, Siskiyou, Sonoma, and Trinity Counties.
[c] Includes Prince William Sound and Copper River basin.
[d] Eleven counties west of the continental divide.
[e] May not add because of rounding.

Sources: See endnote 7. One acre equals 0.405 hectare.

"stumpage" fees charged by the ministry for standing timber have often been insufficient to cover even its own costs.

The Ministry of Forests lost Can$1.1 billion in the six years before 1987, when the threat of import tariffs by the United States (to offset subsidized timber prices) led B.C. to raise its stumpage fees. Since then, provincewide revenues have exceeded the ministry's costs, because profits from two regions, Vancouver and Prince George, have offset losses from four other regions. Other government agencies, including Forestry Canada and Canada's Department of External Affairs (which promotes exports), also extend benefits to the industry. In total, B.C. and Canadian taxpayers provided more than Can$2 billion of support for the province's forest industry in fiscal year 1991–92.[8]

In British Columbia, the provincial government has a near monopoly on timber supplies, controlling 94 percent of the province's forested land. The fair market value of timber, and therefore the extent to which timber is underpriced by the government, is difficult to determine. One partial indicator is the government's Small Business Forest Enterprise Program, under which about 10 percent of the province's timber is sold. Stumpage fees determined by public auction under this program are two to three times higher than the administratively set fees paid by major forest-products companies in B.C. In part, the prices differ because large companies pay some of the costs of building logging roads on Crown lands, whereas the government builds logging roads for small businesses.[9]

How much of the price difference is due to road costs and how much is a subsidy has been a subject of international dispute. In 1994, responding to rising global prices for timber and to U.S. complaints that Canada unfairly subsidized its timber exports, the Ministry of Forests nearly doubled stumpage rates. To some degree, this move reduced the subsidy to the forest sector, but industry's net payments to the province will not rise as steeply because stumpage fees are tax deductible. And much of the increased revenue will go toward implementation of the province's new forest practices code and a new jobs program for unemployed loggers, rather than to general revenues. Arguably, these costs arose because past overcutting led to environmental damage and layoffs. Had industry been forced to pay market prices all along—and follow at least minimal environmental standards—the incentive for overcutting on Crown lands would have been less, some of these costs would have been avoided, and present government deficits would be smaller.[10]

As in B.C., the public owns much of the U.S. Northwest forest. The most egregious subsidies to the U.S. timber industry occur in the Tongass National Forest, which covers four-fifths of southeast Alaska and is the largest national forest in the United States. The U.S. Forest Service has for decades supervised the liquidation of old-growth rain forest in the Tongass, at great expense to the U.S. Treasury. Under 50-year contracts signed in the 1950s, two pulp mill companies were guaranteed monopoly access to nearby timber and large quantities of timber for as little as US$1.48 per thousand board feet; at that price, the wood needed to build the average American house would cost about $15. Congress passed a law in 1990 aimed at reducing these subsidies and the mismanagement of the forest. Yet the Tongass continues to drain the federal treasury, losing $40 million on timber sales in 1993. The Tongass sells more timber, and loses more money, than any other national forest.[11]

Unusual subsidies also spurred the elimination of old-growth forest on much of the half-million acres of land held by southeast Alaskan native corporations. Under legal provisions designed to enable native groups with little business experience to compete against outside firms, the corporations could sell timber at a loss, yet make a profit by selling their financial losses to outside firms; the firms could then use these losses to reduce their own taxable income and tax payments. This highly unusual system was eliminated in 1988, but not before much of southeast Alaska's best forest land had been cleared, and many village corporations had run out of timber.[12]

National forests in the U.S. Northwest often sell timber below their cost of providing it (see Table 2). The U.S. Forest Service claims that its timber sale program nets a profit in the region, but it can make this claim only because of its questionable accounting methods. The Forest Service's Timber Sale Program Information Reporting System (TSPIRS) departs widely from private-sector accounting practices, omitting the costs of excavating and grading logging roads, a major expense in the Northwest's mountainous and often remote national forests. With these costs included, logging of Northwest national forests cost taxpayers some $91 million in 1993.[13]

National forests on the west side of the Cascades have traditionally been big moneymakers for the government. In these lush old-growth forests, timber sales—cashing in the result of centuries of photosynthesis—actually made money. But even where it earns a profit, government can still fail to capture the fair market value of the timber

Table 2. Revenues from Logging in National Forests in the U.S. Northwest, 1993

Region	TSPIRS[a] Net Revenue (million U.S. dollars)	Actual Net Revenue[b]	Volume Harvested (million board feet)
Idaho	19.8	-11.7	570
Oregon			
Eastside	109.8	66.6	1,010
Westside	9.9	-22.9	300
Washington			
Eastside	-10.1	-21.0	160
Westside	-3.2	-24.6	190
Northwest California[c]	-2.4	-18.7	140
Southeast Alaska[d]	-14.5	-41.0	330
Western Montana[e]	4.5	-17.5	300
Total[f]	113.9	-90.9	3,000

[a] Timber Sale Program Information Reporting System of the U.S. Forest Service.
[b] Subtracts road-building costs and allocated share of timber program-office costs from TSPIRS figures.
[c] Includes Klamath, Shasta-Trinity, and Six Rivers National Forests.
[d] Includes Tongass and Chugach National Forests.
[e] Includes Bitterroot, Deerlodge, Flathead, Kootenai, and Lolo National Forests.
[f] May not add because of rounding.
Sources: See endnote 13. One U.S. dollar equaled 1.29 Canadian dollars in 1993.
One million board feet (logs) equals roughly 3500 cubic meters.

it sells. Competitive bidding determines timber prices, but the Forest Service does not consider its own costs when determining the minimum acceptable bid, often well below market value. And BLM, which manages 830,000 acres (340,000 hectares) of forest in southwestern Oregon, sells most of its timber by oral auction, which nets lower returns than sealed bidding. At any rate, few old-growth forests remain on the Westside; this decline, in combination with tougher environmental protection measures, has put these forests' timber programs below cost as well.[14]

In a handful of cases, the Forest Service has established "sustained-yield units" from which only local mills may buy timber, thereby reducing competition (and prices) for timber. In the Olympic National Forest's Shelton Unit—a thoroughly worked-over landscape of logging roads, clearcuts, and young tree farms—timber is usually sold at its appraised price. Outside the unit, timber usually sells at 10 to 50 percent above the appraised price, indicating just how far below market value Shelton Unit timber is priced.[15]

Timber companies also receive subsidies in the form of generous tax breaks. In the United States, "limited partnerships" that earn 90 percent of their income from timber, minerals, fertilizer, or geothermal energy are exempt from paying corporate income taxes. Plum Creek Timber Company, owner of 1.4 million acres (570,000 hectares) of land in the U.S. Northwest and the largest private owner of grizzly bear habitat in the country, became a limited partnership in mid-1989. Reportedly, the company paid $14 million in state and federal taxes on $24 million in income in the first five months of 1989. In the next seven months, it paid only $400,000 in taxes on $14 million in income. Plum Creek has been responsible for some of the worst forest overcutting in the region. Other timber firms taking advantage of this tax break in the Northwest include International Paper and ITT.[16]

LOGGING OF NATIONAL FORESTS IN THE NORTHWEST COST TAXPAYERS SOME $91 MILLION IN 1993.

Canadian forest-products companies benefit from a variety of tax breaks, including reduced assessments on the taxable value of forest lands and a 10 percent reduction from federal business tax rates; this discount saves B.C. firms some Can$40 million per year. Most significant, timber producers are allowed to defer federal tax payments based on their investment in capital equipment—for a savings to B.C. firms of an estimated Can$2 billion in 1991. This equipment-based tax relief not only gives firms an incentive to overproduce but also lowers the cost of capital relative to labor, encouraging firms to replace workers with machinery.[17]

The Oregon legislature handed the state timber industry a handsome discount on its tax payments in 1993. Oregon lawmakers virtually eliminated property taxes on private forest lands by slashing the land's assessed value. Under the new law, almost all timber land in southern Oregon's Josephine County is valued for tax purposes at less than $42 an acre; more than half is valued at less than $7 an acre. Statewide, 30,000 acres (12,000 hectares) of timber land will be taxed at a value of $1 per acre and another 200,000 (80,000 hectares) at only $7 an acre. Timber companies in the state will save an estimated $87 million annually by 1998 as this and other tax breaks take effect—roughly a 60 percent tax cut, despite the $600 million budget deficit faced by the state government.[18]

One of the farthest reaching subsidies to affect Northwest forests goes not to the timber industry but to homeowners. Under the U.S. tax code, homeowners can deduct all property tax and mortgage interest from their federal income taxes. Though this tax break has a laudable purpose—encouraging home ownership—its effect has been to provide a tax shelter that disproportionately benefits the wealthy, giving them an incentive to buy larger, and more, houses than they need. Housing construction is the single largest user of lumber in North America; the rapid spread of residential developments (often second homes) in suburban or more remote settings is also consuming natural habitats and worsening car-based pollution across the Northwest (see "Sprawl," p. 41). Low- and moderate-income taxpayers, who are less likely to itemize their deductions and more likely to be renters, are often unable to take advantage of the mortgage deduction. Canada has no such income tax break, yet its rate of homeownership is the same as that in the United States.[19]

Nationwide, this deduction cost the federal government US$41 billion in lost tax revenues in 1993, more than the entire budget of the

Department of Housing and Urban Development. In effect, wealthy homeowners receive far more in housing assistance than do the homeless. Five-sixths of the tax savings went to the richest 25 percent of U.S. taxpayers: those who earn more than $50,000 a year. According to the Congressional Budget Office, eliminating mortgage interest deductions for second homes would save about $300 million annually nationwide; capping the deduction at $12,000 per person (which would affect only the wealthiest 2 percent of taxpayers) would save $1.7 billion each year.[20]

WEALTHY HOMEOWNERS RECEIVE FAR MORE IN HOUSING ASSISTANCE THAN DO THE HOMELESS.

Subsidies to the forest products industry concentrate benefits on a relative handful of companies and squander the natural capital of Northwest forests. Even those forms of subsidy that appear most democratic, such as the mortgage interest tax deduction, preferentially benefit those fully capable of paying the costs of their demand for wood. Subsidies for logging old-growth timber harm the industry itself by penalizing the handful of firms working to use their forests in ecologically sound ways—to give both their industry and the environment a decent future.

MINING

No sector of the Northwest economy is subsidized more generously than the mining industry. Governments sell many resources at a discount and, in the U.S. Northwest, simply give water away free. But only the General Mining Law of 1872, signed by U.S. President Ulysses S. Grant, gives away both resources *and* the land that holds them. Under this law, any citizen or business (including subsidiaries of foreign corporations) has the right to take gold, silver, copper, and other hardrock minerals from public land for free and can also purchase land lying above a mineral deposit for a nominal fee. Holding sway long after its usefulness has ended, the 1872 Mining Law stands out as the most archaic of Wilkinson's "lords of yesterday."

The 1872 law, originally intended to spur miners to take their mules and axes and settle the West, made mining the favored use of public land in the western United States, except where specifically prohibited. Today citizens and corporations have a "right to mine" on most public lands in the West: miners, not land managers, decide what lands should or should not be mined. After staking a claim and spending $100 (in labor or, more recently, in cash) on the claim per year, miners have the right to sell minerals from the land without paying any royalties to the government, which owns the land. One hundred dollars in 1872 was nearly two months' wages; today, the fee (though raised to $225 in 1994) is a trivial sum, especially compared with the value of minerals being given away.[21]

In addition, the law allows holders of claims to "patent" (a legal term for purchase) land where minerals are found for $2.50 or $5.00 an acre. Again, $5 was a sizeable amount in the nineteenth century; today it is laughable. Such a low price provides a huge incentive to purchase the land and resell it for other uses—a common practice. In

1989, Harold Duval and his family patented 780 acres (320 hectares) of sand dunes in the Oregon Dunes National Recreation Area at $2.50 an acre, paying $1,950 in total. (In addition to hardrock minerals, "uncommon" varieties of common minerals, such as contaminant-free sand, are also covered under the 1872 law.) Seeking to reacquire the area, the U.S. Forest Service has offered the Duvals other parcels of Forest Service land worth approximately $2 million in exchange for their patented property; the Duvals have refused, demanding a price of $12 million.[22]

Normally, genuine miners have little incentive to patent the land since mining can proceed unfettered without patenting. But the prospect of legal reform in the early 1990s sent many companies rushing to patent their claims—and obtain inviolable property rights—before the Mining Act might be updated. In 1994, more than 80 patents under the Mining Act were pending in Northwest states. Canada's Noranda Minerals Company is seeking the region's largest patent, for the Montanore mine in northwestern Montana. The patent would transfer nearly $4 billion in copper and silver to Noranda; it would also make a large bloc of Montana's federally protected Cabinet Mountains Wilderness Area, critical habitat for the endangered grizzly bear, the private property of a multinational mining company (see Table 3).[23]

The full extent of taxpayer losses if pending patents are approved— and the full extent of past losses of minerals and lands under the act—

Table 3. Four Largest Mining Patents Pending in the U.S. Northwest, 1994

Mine Name and Location	Mineral	Patent Price	Estimated Mineral Value[a]
Montanore, Montana	Copper, silver	$185	$3.69 billion
Crown Jewel, Washington	Gold	$1,380	$570 million
Grouse Creek, Idaho	Gold, silver	$2,230	$379 million
Grassy Mountain, Oregon	Gold, silver	$310	$155 million

[a] Current value of recoverable mineral reserve being patented.

Source: Thomas J. Hilliard et al., Golden Patents, Empty Pockets (Washington, D.C.: Mineral Policy Center, 1994).

is unknown. The federal government has little information on the value of mining on public or formerly public lands. A reasonable estimate of the value of public mineral assets given away in the Northwest is in the tens of billions of dollars; the revenue lost by failing to charge royalties on hardrock minerals likely comes to the hundreds of millions. In contrast, producers of other types of minerals in the United States pay substantial royalties. The government charges royalties of 12.5 percent on oil and gas, at least 12 percent on surface-mined coal, and 10 to 15 percent on geothermal steam.[24]

British Columbia collects no royalties on minerals, though more minerals are extracted there than anywhere else in the Northwest, and the provincial government actively promotes mineral development on its lands. The B.C. government spends Can$1.6 million annually on minerals research and development and, in 1994, started the Explore B.C. program of roughly Can$4 million annually in grants for mineral exploration. It is hard to say whether B.C. mining companies receive unfair tax breaks compared with other sectors, or whether taxes are sufficient to make up for the lack of royalties. Corporate taxes are complex and controversial in Canada, with various industries benefiting from various loopholes. For years, mining companies could avoid paying federal taxes by reinvesting the taxes owed in their mining projects, but this allowance was discontinued in 1991.[25]

The Mining Association of British Columbia argues that B.C. miners pay higher taxes than competitors in other nations. U.S. miners, for example, receive generous tax exemptions in the form of "depletion allowances": they can deduct from 5 to 22 percent of their gross income when figuring their taxes. Intended to compensate miners for exhaustion of nonrenewable capital stock, the allowances actually provide an incentive to deplete the resource.[26]

Hardrock mines often discharge acids, heavy metals, and other toxic substances into their surroundings. Yet the mining industry is exempt from the main federal law regulating hazardous wastes (the

Resource Conservation and Recovery Act); the 1872 Mining Law requires no remediation of old mining sites. British Columbia and many U.S. states, by contrast, require operators to post bonds to ensure that mining sites are restored. The bonds are sometimes insufficient to cover reclamation costs, and cleanup requirements are not always enforced, but these programs are far stronger than provisions of the 1872 act. In any event, whenever government fails to push miners to clean up their sites, or when mining companies declare bankruptcy, the government itself ends up providing the service at taxpayer expense. Hardrock mining has left the Northwest with the two largest Superfund hazardous waste sites in the United States: the first 140 miles (90 kilometers) of the Clark Fork River (downstream from the closed copper mines around Butte, Montana) and Lake Coeur d'Alene (the final resting place for toxic sediments from Idaho's Silver Valley). Cleaning up mining areas on the Superfund National Priorities List of hazardous waste sites will cost at least $100 million in the U.S. Northwest; sites not on the Superfund list will cost at least a billion more (see Table 4).[27]

Environmental damage varies from mineral to mineral and by mining method. Many common and little-subsidized materials such as stone, sand, and gravel are usually dug from shallow deposits and used with minimal processing; their extraction has few impacts beyond

Table 4. Remediation Cost Estimates for Abandoned Mines in the U.S. Northwest

Region	Superfund Sites (million U.S. dollars)	All Known Sites (million U.S. dollars)
Idaho	5–10	315
Oregon	17	69–89
Washington	20–118	Unknown
Montana[a]	58	912
Northwest California	5	Unknown

[a] Entire state.

Sources: See endnote 27.

disturbance of the immediate site. The heavily subsidized hardrock minerals are usually dug from deeper and lower-grade ores that require extensive processing, which demands large amounts of energy and often pollutes heavily (see "Electricity," p. 32). The average copper ore mined today, for example, contains less than 1 percent copper; in other words, 99 percent of the rock removed from a copper mine becomes waste.[28]

Gold, however, is in a class by itself when it comes to environmental impact per unit of output. Gold ores mined today average 0.00033 percent metal: producing one gram of gold requires digging through, processing, and dumping 3 million grams (roughly 3 tons) of earth. Mining such low-grade ores was made feasible by taxpayer-funded

PRODUCING ONE GRAM OF GOLD REQUIRES DIGGING THROUGH, PROCESSING, AND DUMPING 3 MILLION GRAMS OF EARTH.

research by the U.S. Bureau of Mines. The Bureau pioneered several now widespread mineral extraction processes, including the cyanide heap leach technology used in large Northwest gold mines. Cyanide leaking from gold mines in Idaho has polluted salmon streams and killed hundreds of migratory birds.[29]

The 1872 Mining Law was intended to benefit the small miner struggling to make a living, and the mining industry still invokes this image in the law's defense. But the billions of dollars subsidizing mineral development actually benefit few people. Modern mining is the province of multinational firms that employ relatively few workers and invest heavily in sophisticated machinery, energy, and chemicals to unearth and process vast quantities of raw materials. Even a half century ago, Franklin Roosevelt's Secretary of the Interior Harold Ickes pointed out, "The individual prospector no longer exists as a significant factor in the mining industry." Subsidies to this industry take money away from other economic sectors that employ more people and have less impact on the earth.[30]

AGRICULTURE

Governments assist agriculture through price supports, low-interest loans, import restrictions, disaster insurance, and numerous other programs. Many of these, born in the Great Depression, have helped reduce the numbers of farmers forced out of business in lean economic times since. Yet many programs now primarily benefit large-scale farmers and agribusiness firms at the expense of taxpayers and small farmers.[31]

The two key environmentally harmful incentives to agriculture in the Northwest are underpriced water and grazing rights. Irrigation, a central feature of Northwest agriculture (see Table 5), uses far more water than all other activities in the region. In Idaho, Oregon, and Washington, farmers withdraw ten times as much water as all other users combined. Idaho irrigators, for example, divert the entire flow of the Snake River at Milner Dam; until recently, the state of Idaho considered any water that made it over the dam "wasted."[32]

Farmers can afford to use so much water because they pay so little for it. Under western water law, with its doctrine of "prior appropriation," water belongs to the state but is free for the taking to the first party that diverts it for "beneficial use." This nineteenth-century doctrine has effectively given entire rivers to irrigators across the western United States. It has made possible water use on an industrial scale—at no charge—by thousands of private users and by a small number of large, publicly built irrigation projects. Of all publicly owned natural resources in the Pacific Northwest, only water (in the United States) and minerals are given away absolutely free.[33]

Though water itself is free, irrigators pay to have it stored in reservoirs and delivered by canals. The U.S. Bureau of Reclamation, created in 1902 to help small farmers settle the arid West, has built irrigation projects along the Klamath, Snake, and Yakima Rivers and elsewhere in the Northwest, largely at public expense. Under the Bureau's original legislation, only small farmers could participate, and they were to repay the costs of the dams and reservoirs within ten years. In practice, large farms receive most of the benefits and very few of the costs are repaid by irrigators, leaving taxpayers with most of the bill.[34]

As Congress lengthened farmers' repayment period from ten to forty or fifty years, the initially innocuous decision to charge them no interest has resulted in an enormous subsidy. Moreover, if the Bureau deems a farmer's "ability to pay" insufficient, then the interest-free loan payments are reduced even further. Because of these factors, the U.S. Department of the Interior has calculated that 86 percent of Bureau of Reclamation irrigation project costs are never actually repaid. In addition, the Bureau's accounting inflates the nonirrigation portions of its projects (such as recreation or flood control), whose costs are absorbed by the government. In fact, federal taxpayers cover 90 percent or more of the cost of delivering Bureau of Reclamation water to farmers.[35]

In eastern Washington, the Bureau's Columbia Basin Project (CBP) provides water and power to half a million acres of some of the most

Table 5. The Scale of Irrigated Agriculture in the Pacific Northwest, 1992

Region	Area (thousand acres)	Share of Cropland (percent)	Share of Water Withdrawals (percent)
Idaho	3,260	52	92
Washington	1,640	21	71
Oregon	1,620	32	88
Western Montana	360	57	Unknown
British Columbia[a]	230	17	25
Northwest California	190	44	Unknown
Total	7,310[b]	34	86

[a] 1990 data.
[b] May not add because of rounding.
Sources: See endnote 32. One acre equals 0.405 hectare.

Table 6. Federal Subsidies to the Columbia Basin Project

Category	Subsidy Estimate
Project construction	$109–225 million since 1940
Construction interest	$3.2 billion since 1940
Pumping discount	$25 million per year
Drainage system construction	$150 million since 1960
Lost hydropower potential	$80–130 million per year
In-canal hydropower	$850,000 per year

Sources: See endnote 36.

lavishly subsidized farms anywhere (see Table 6). Encompassing Grand Coulee Dam and large networks of canals and pumps, CBP lifts water uphill from the Columbia River and distributes it practically free to farms averaging 500 acres in size. In 1988, the Interior Department estimated that the average subsidy to a 960-acre farm in CBP totaled more than $2 million. In addition, farmers pay $912,000 annually for hydropower to pump water; at the wholesale rates paid by other users of power from Grand Coulee, that power is worth more than $25 million annually. Water is pumped uphill so cheaply, and in such volumes, that some irrigators have built their *own* hydroelectric plants in CBP canals to make money on the resulting downhill flow. Irrigators sell $850,000 of electricity to local utilities annually. Other irrigators served by the Bonneville Power Administration (BPA), and those served by B.C. Hydro, receive special discounts on power prices, but none are as deep as CBP's.[36]

The largest Bureau of Reclamation project in the U.S., the Minidoka Project, covers one million acres of Idaho's Snake River Plain. Farmers pay about $2.50 per acre-foot of water from the Minidoka Project—or about a penny for 1,300 gallons. An acre-foot of water left in the river at Minidoka Dam could produce $46 to $106 of hydropower on its way to the sea; households in Boise pay $350 to $440 per acre-foot for tap water. Water diverted to farmers by the

Minidoka Project would generate at least $80 million more each year for the regional economy if it were left in the river. For the Columbia River basin as a whole, BPA has estimated the cost of hydropower foregone because of water consumed by irrigation at more than $200 million annually.[37]

The subsidies themselves are tremendous, but more perverse, many of them pay farmers to produce the same crops that they and other farmers are paid *not* to produce. In the 1980s, the federal government paid Idaho farmers roughly $150 million a year not to grow wheat and barley, which are produced in surplus. One-third of the Minidoka's acreage grows wheat and barley; and more than one-third of the water drawn from the Snake River by the Bureau of Reclamation is used for these surplus crops. As author Tim Palmer writes in *The Snake River*, "Everyone in our society is subsidized in one way or another, but few people are subsidized to produce a product while at the same time being subsidized to not produce it."[38]

The impacts of subsidized irrigation are not limited to water consumption. Along with power production, providing water to farmers was a driving force behind the government-funded damming of the Columbia and Snake Rivers and the collapse of salmon runs in the Columbia Basin. Even farmers who do not rely on irrigation—such as the wheat farmers of eastern Washington's rapidly eroding Palouse Hills—benefit from dams. Dams and locks have turned the Columbia and lower Snake Rivers into a freeway for ocean-going ships as far as 700 miles (1,100 kilometers) upriver; one-third of all U.S. wheat exports are carried down the Columbia. Shippers pay none of the U.S. Army Corps of Engineers' costs for operating and maintaining the locks and dams or for dredging the navigational channel, which cost $30 million in 1994. In 1994, the Corps also

MANY SUBSIDIES PAY FARMERS TO PRODUCE THE SAME CROPS THAT THEY AND OTHER FARMERS ARE PAID NOT TO PRODUCE.

provided half the funding for a $6 million study to determine the feasibility of dredging the first 110 miles (180 kilometers) of the Columbia three feet deeper. The project, expected to cost $100 million, would enable fully loaded oceangoing vessels to use the river all summer long; its effects on aquatic life are unknown.[39]

When compared with other environmentally harmful subsidies, the fiscal losses associated with below-cost grazing are not steep. But the economic activity that grazing subsidies support degrades the environment across broad areas of the Northwest. Mountainous British Columbia devotes relatively little area to agriculture, other than livestock grazing. Ten percent of the province—an area about half the size of Idaho—supports cattle and sheep, mostly on Crown lands (see Table 7). As in the rest of the Northwest, livestock have altered practically every acre of grass-growing land.[40]

Throughout the Northwest, government consistently undercharges for the right to run livestock on public land. BLM, which manages a large share of Northwest dry lands, consistently charges too little to

Table 7. The Scale of Grazing in the Pacific Northwest, 1992

Region	Public Land Used for Grazing[a] (million acres)	Private Land Used for Grazing (million acres)	Grazing's Share of Total Land Area (percent)
British Columbia	21.0	3.1	10
Idaho	14.7	7.5	42
Oregon	13.8	12.5	42
Washington	1.1	7.5	20
Northwest California	0.1[b]	2.0	16
Southeast Alaska	0.0	0.0	0
Western Montana	0.4	2.6	19
Total[c]	52.1	35.2	19

[a] Does not include U.S. Forest Service land used for grazing.
[b] Does not include land owned by the state of California.
[c] May not add because of rounding.

Sources: See endnote 40. One acre equals 0.405 hectare.

recover the costs of administering grazing on its lands. BLM charges
$1.98 per animal–unit–month (AUM: the amount a cow and calf eat
in a month, equaling about 800 pounds of forage) and loses about
$3 million annually in the Pacific Northwest (see Table 8). The cost
borne by ranchers is even less than $1.98 per AUM because half of
BLM grazing revenues are used to pay for projects, such as building
water tanks for cattle in remote spots, that directly benefit grazing
permit holders. In 1994, Interior Secretary Bruce Babbitt sought to
more than double grazing fees on BLM lands but abandoned the
effort in the face of resistance from western ranchers and legislators.[41]

BLM charges far less for grazing rights than do private landowners
and less than most state land agencies. Only the B.C Ministry of
Forests (which administers grazing on Crown lands) charges less (see
Table 9). Some of this difference can be explained by BLM requirements that grazing permit holders maintain fencing and water sources
for livestock. But ranchers often sublease their BLM permits at a profit
and benefit from increases in the value of private property associated

Table 8. Net Revenue from Grazing on Federal and Provincial Land in
the Pacific Northwest, 1992

Region	Revenue	Expenditures[a] (thousand U.S. dollars)	Net Revenue
British Columbia	1,729	5,294	−3,564
Idaho	1,981	3,785	−1,804
Oregon	1,360	2,789	−1,428
Washington	47	96	−48
Northwest California	15	29	−14
Western Montana	14	72	−58
Total[b]	5,146	12,066	−6,916

[a] U.S. figures for Bureau of Land Management only. Expenditures include portion of BLM
budget allocated to grazing fee administration, the 12.5–50 percent of revenue returned to
states and counties, and the 50 percent spent on range improvement. B.C. expenditures from
Ministry of Forests Range Branch budget.
[b] May not add because of rounding.
Sources: See endnote 41. One U.S. dollar equaled 1.21 Canadian dollars in 1992.

Table 9. Grazing Fees in the Pacific Northwest, 1994

Region	BLM Fee	State or Provincial Fee	Average Private Fee
		(U.S. dollars per animal-unit-month)	
British Columbia	–	1.50	Unknown
Idaho	1.98	5.15[a]	9.70
Oregon	1.98	2.50–3.50	9.00
Washington	1.98	4.73–7.15	8.30
Northwest California	1.98	1.93	11.00
Western Montana	1.98	4.61[a]	11.80

[a] Fee for 1995.

Sources: See endnote 42. One U.S. dollar equaled 1.35 Canadian dollars in 1994.

with grazing allotments—both indicators that BLM fees fall well below market value. Even the higher state fees are well below market value. An uproar ensued when Jon Marvel of the Idaho Watersheds Project, a local environmental group, entered the market and outbid local ranchers at an auction for a grazing permit on state land. Marvel intended to pay for the right to let the area recover from livestock impacts. The state lands board overturned his winning bid.[42]

As with many agricultural subsidies, the original intent of low grazing fees has been subverted. Grazing subsidies benefit a small number of increasingly large landholders, rather than the large number of small landholders originally intended. Nationwide, 10 percent of BLM permitees control 75 percent of BLM's total grazing area. The J.R. Simplot Company of Boise, one of the 250 largest corporations in the U.S., controls 1.7 million acres (700,000 hectares) of BLM grazing permits in Idaho, Nevada, Oregon, and Utah. Even when agricultural subsidies reach small farmers, projects may be so costly that their net effect is to hurt the poor. The Columbia Basin Project, for example, takes more money from low-income taxpayers nationwide than it distributes to low-income farm families in the project.[43]

The most straightforward subsidies to agriculture—direct income-support payments for farmers—are less damaging ecologically than subsidies to irrigation and grazing, though they impose major fiscal burdens. U.S. commodity programs, Canada's "supply management," and other measures designed to control the price and supply of selected crops constitute a sizeable fraction of total income for many farmers. Farmers in the U.S. Northwest received $236 million in income supports in 1992; direct payments to B.C. farmers totaled Can$51 million in 1992. Environmental impacts from this complex web of financial supports are mixed. Some programs tend to reduce environmental impacts by limiting overproduction; others take on farmers' costs or risks and encourage overproduction. U.S. commodity programs discourage crop rotation and other environmentally beneficial farming practices by essentially requiring participating farmers to plant the same crops year after year to receive benefits. Like subsidies to irrigation and livestock grazing, payments are skewed toward large farms: 40 percent of all income-support payments go to the 5 percent of farmers with the largest farms. Whether commodity programs or below-cost water and grazing rights, tax dollars are being funneled to a shrinking number of increasingly propped-up farms operating in ecologically unsound ways.[44]

ELECTRICITY

Naturally powerful rivers and copious government subsidies provide northwesterners with abundant and exceptionally cheap electricity. Hundreds of dams blocking rivers in the Columbia Basin and elsewhere make the Pacific Northwest a world center of hydro-power production, and the region has some of the highest electricity consumption rates in the world. Hydropower provides 80 percent of the Northwest's electricity and 39 percent of its overall energy use.[45]

Electricity prices in the Pacific Northwest are lower than in the rest of the United States or Canada (see Table 10). Overall, prices are lowest in British Columbia, which never invested in costly nuclear energy. Electricity rates in the U.S. Northwest were even lower before the Washington Public Power Supply System (WPPSS) began a massive nuclear power construction program in the 1970s. WPPSS failed, leaving BPA, the Northwest's largest supplier of power, with billions of dollars in debt. BPA increased its rates sevenfold in the early 1980s as it took responsibility for the failed nuclear program. Today, roughly 15 to 25 percent of every residential electric bill in the U.S. Northwest pays for one inefficient and two never-completed nuclear power plants in Washington. Even so, electricity prices for BPA customers are still about half the national average.[46]

Created during the New Deal to market power from U.S. Army Corps of Engineers and Bureau of Reclamation dams in the Columbia Basin, BPA was chartered to encourage the widest possible use of electricity at the lowest possible price. Today it distributes from 30 federally built dams and one nuclear plant roughly one-half of all the energy consumed in Idaho, Montana, Oregon, and Washington. Though legally required to repay the costs of dam construction and operation out of power revenue, BPA still charges low electric rates and pays the federal government only a fraction of what it owes.[47]

Subsidies to electricity users through BPA, which total hundreds of millions of dollars annually and speed the decline of salmon runs in the heavily dammed Columbia Basin, are among the costliest antienvironmental handouts in the Pacific Northwest. Estimates of the subsidy range between $200 million and $1 billion per year, depending on assumptions made in calculation. At a minimum, BPA undercharges its customers $213 million per year, based on the difference between BPA prices and those charged by private (investor-owned) utilities in its service area.[48]

Based on BPA's cost of providing electricity from federal dams, the subsidy is much greater. If BPA had to repay its loans for dam construction at market rates (either the rate private utilities pay or the government's bond rate, rather than federally subsidized interest rates), it would have to charge its customers $590 to $720 million more per year. To earn the same rate of return as private utilities, BPA would have to charge its customers $1.18 billion more per year than at present. In addition, nationwide subsidies to the nuclear industry (including research and development and caps on liability for accidents and nuclear waste cleanup) translate into a subsidy to BPA's sole operating nuclear

Table 10. Pacific Northwest Electricity Prices and Consumption, 1992

Region	Residential and Commercial (U.S. cents per kilowatt–hour)	Industrial	Per Capita Use (kWh/year)
Canadian Average	5.5	3.4	16,700
British Columbia	4.5	1.9	14,600
U.S. Average	8.0	4.8	11,100
Idaho	4.6	2.7	17,800
Oregon	4.9	3.2	14,400
Washington	4.4	2.2	17,400
Western Montana[a]	5.2	2.6	25,100

[a] 1990 figures.

Sources: See endnote 46. One U.S. dollar equaled 1.21 Canadian dollars in 1992.

plant of $6 to $15 million per year. Every U.S. president since Jimmy Carter has sought to refinance BPA's debt at higher interest rates (thereby reducing government losses and increasing electricity prices), but Northwest congressional delegations have consistently blocked these efforts.[49]

Electricity prices in British Columbia are exceptionally low. This situation apparently reflects the province's steep, high-volume rivers and its refusal to pursue nuclear energy, although government subsidies also play a role. B.C. Hydro, the tax-exempt government corporation that generates 85 percent of the electricity consumed in the province, makes a profit and pays a dividend to the provincial government. The utility carries Can$7 billion in debt on hydroelectric dams built with government financing. This debt is being repaid at market rates, but the provincial government's guarantee of B.C. Hydro's debt enables the utility to borrow at lower rates than otherwise. The value of the government's assumption of the utility's financial risk is unknown.[50]

Though almost all northwesterners benefit from cheap electricity (see Table 10), some are more heavily subsidized than others. One industry in particular—aluminum smelting—enjoys the largest subsidies. Aluminum smelters, which purchase roughly one-third of all electricity sold by BPA, are charged special low rates in exchange for using much of their electricity at night, when demand is low, and for agreeing to allow the agency to shut off their power with little notice. Though this "interruptible power" is worth less than "firm power" (which cannot be shut off), BPA sells the power below its cost and market value. BPA's cost of providing electricity to the smelters over the past decade exceeded its revenue by about $100 million per year. In 1994, BPA's lost revenue came to approximately $130 to $170 million. Other BPA customers are charged more to recoup this loss: aluminum subsidies cost the average household served by BPA about $2 per month.[51]

British Columbia's only aluminum smelter, the Alcan smelter at Kitimat in northern B.C., is more heavily subsidized than those supplied by BPA. Alcan reroutes water from an inland reservoir through a tunnel in the Coast Range to its hydropower plant on the coast. The company pays the province water-rental fees well below those that other hydro producers must pay—yielding Alcan a windfall worth approximately Can$26 million a year. In addition, B.C. gives Alcan generous tax breaks: all land under Alcan's reservoir, dam, power plant, smelter, and company town is exempt from property taxes.[52]

One of the world's most energy-intensive industries, aluminum smelting places heavy demands on Northwest rivers. Though water falling past turbines, not fossil fuel, powers aluminum production in the Northwest, the industry also emits large amounts of carbon dioxide and other greenhouse gases. Electric current flows through carbon electrodes in the final stage of aluminum production, releasing two pounds of carbon dioxide for every pound of aluminum produced.[53]

Aluminum—dubbed "congealed electricity"—is so energy intensive that the easiest way to conserve electricity in the Northwest would be to produce (and consume) less of the metal. But because power is so heavily subsidized, major savings could also be realized by simply improving the efficiency of energy use within aluminum smelters. Washington's eight smelters, which produce about a third of U.S. aluminum output, are 14 percent less efficient in their use of electricity than the world average (see Table 11). Yet low power prices discourage

Table 11. Electricity Consumption of Pacific Northwest Aluminum Smelters, 1993

Region	Consumption per Metric Ton[a] of Aluminum Produced (kilowatt-hour)
British Columbia	19,600
Washington	17,900
North America	16,000
World Average	15,700

[a] One metric ton equals 2,200 pounds.
Sources: See endnote 54.

Washington's older smelters from making capital investments to improve energy efficiency.[54]

Both BPA and the B.C. government tie hydropower prices charged to smelters to the world market price of aluminum. Though the rates paid by B.C.'s Alcan are kept secret, one government observer estimates that the company pays 95 percent less than other hydropower generators in B.C. for the use of water. In 1987, Alcan reported paying a rate for water equivalent to 0.7 Canadian cents per kilowatt-hour of electricity generated, less than one-fourth the rate that subsidized smelters were charged by BPA. Without these uniquely cheap rates, Alcan's smelter—one of the least efficient in the world—would probably not be in business.[55]

Hatcheries

Salmon hatcheries are often viewed as a form of assistance to the fishing industry: they put fish in the water for fleets to catch without charge. But in the Columbia River basin, government spending on hatcheries can more accurately be categorized as a subsidy to electricity use. The more than 80 salmon hatcheries now operating in the basin were funded largely by state and federal governments to mitigate the impacts of government-built hydroelectric dams on wild salmon runs. In the 1980s, government agencies paid $54 million per year to operate the hatcheries.[56]

Despite the release of increasing numbers of salmon fry from these hatcheries, the number of adult fish returning to the Columbia has plummeted, and the number of wild salmon has fallen even more, by 96 to 98 percent. Rather than offsetting the dams' toll, hatcheries exacerbate it: hatchery fish compete with, interbreed with, and promote overfishing of wild salmon. More important, they have helped hydropower producers and consumers avoid for years their obligations to protect salmon stocks, thereby shifting the costs of electricity consumption onto the fishing industry, Indian tribes, and all Northwest citizens who suffer from the loss of salmon. Because of the operation of hydroelectric dams and their reservoirs, the Columbia remains a dangerous place for salmon.[57]

CARS

by Rhys Roth

T ransportation in the Pacific Northwest, as in the rest of Canada and the United States, is dominated by the private automobile and its close relatives—vans, pickup trucks, and recreational vehicles. Northwesterners make fully 90 percent of their trips by car or truck.[58]

The region's dependence on automobiles may seem natural enough: other modes of transportation are seldom as convenient. But driving is the easiest way to get around because of a half century of massive government subsidies. Drivers require roads and bridges, parking facilities, and a variety of government services, but they pay only part of the associated costs through fuel taxes, vehicle registration and license fees, parking charges, and other fees on driving. The rest of the tab is picked up by taxpayers.

The most visible public investment in automobile infrastructure is the US$4 billion spent each year to expand and maintain the region's network of roads and bridges. Public roads and streets now span 234,000 miles (374,000 kilometers) of Idaho, Oregon, and Washington, enough to circle the globe nine times.[59]

In 1992, local, regional, and federal governments spent more than $3.9 billion on Northwest roads (see Table 12). Drivers paid directly about 76 percent of these funds, just less than $3 billion, through gas taxes, vehicle registration and license fees, and other fees charged to road users. The other 24 percent of the roadwork costs, $938 million, came from sources unrelated to driving, including property taxes and general fund appropriations.[60]

North American drivers pay a much smaller share of the costs of driving than drivers in other countries. Canadian gasoline taxes are the second lowest in the industrialized world; only U.S. gas taxes are lower. Because of these low taxes, motor fuel prices in the U.S. and Canada are lower than in any other industrialized country, less than half the

Table 12. Subsidies to Road Construction in the Pacific Northwest,[a] 1992

Revenues (million U.S. dollars)		
Fuel and vehicle taxes		
Federal	667	
State and province	2,104	
Local	100	
Tolls	105	
Total revenues		**2,976**

Expenses (million U.S. dollars)		
Road construction	1,820	
Maintenance	1,519	
Other[b]	576	
Total expenses		**3,915**

Net subsidy to drivers		**938**[c]

[a] Data from British Columbia, Idaho, Oregon, and Washington.
[b] Includes administration and interest on bonds.
[c] May not add because of rounding.
Sources: See endnote 60. One U.S. dollar equaled 1.21 Canadian dollars in 1992.

prices paid by drivers in Germany or Japan. With drivers paying so little for the services they require, others must pay more. In Idaho, Oregon, and Washington, roadwork is subsidized by $319 million in property taxes and $166 million in general fund appropriations. To eliminate nonuser payments for roadwork, Northwest authorities would need to increase gasoline taxes by 14 U.S. cents per gallon.[61]

Roads make automobile travel possible, but the region's 11 million vehicles require even more land on which to park between uses. Each vehicle requires on average more than two parking spaces: one at home, one at work, plus a share of commercial parking. Typical parking stalls are 8 to 10 feet wide and 18 to 20 feet deep, totaling 144 to 200 square feet, plus about an equal amount of space dedicated to access lanes. Assuming an average of 300 square feet per stall, and two stalls per vehicle in the region, more than 147,000 acres (60,000 hectares) of Pacific Northwest land may be dedicated to parking.[62]

A survey of workers in King County, Washington (where Seattle is located), found that 71 percent are offered free parking by their employers and another 4.5 percent get parking at a reduced rate. Nationally, numerous sources indicate that at least 90 percent of Americans park for free at work. The value of free parking at government buildings in the greater Vancouver, British Columbia, region alone reaches Can$26 million per year.[63]

The U.S. federal tax code provides a powerful incentive to employers to offer their employees free parking. The cost of providing free parking is tax exempt up to $155 per month per employee; salaries increased by a comparable amount would be fully taxed. In contrast, no more than $60 per month per employee can be deducted by businesses that provide transit passes or carpool vehicles for their workers. According to Donald C. Shoup of the University of California, Los Angeles, "No other fringe benefit is tax exempt when paid for by the employer but taxable when paid for by the employee."[64]

Canadian employers are officially required to report to Revenue Canada the free parking benefits they provide employees. In practice, however, few do, and enforcement is lax, so employer-paid parking is rarely taxed."[65]

No studies have yet been done in the Northwest, but several case studies of employer-paid parking in downtown Los Angeles indicate that the parking subsidy enjoyed by 50,000 solo commuters is worth 16 times more than the federal gasoline tax they pay for fuel used during their commute. UCLA's Shoup recommends a change in the U.S. tax code to require employers that provide free parking to offer their employees a cash-out option: the choice to forego free parking and instead receive in cash the fair market value of the parking benefit. Such a change could reduce solo work commuting by as much as 20 percent, according to Shoup.[66]

Though their costs have never been studied in detail in the Pacific Northwest, auto-related municipal services, such as traffic policing, fire protection, traffic planning and engineering, street repair and maintenance, and traffic lights, may constitute the largest of all subsidies to car use in the region. Stanley Hart, a civil engineer from Pasadena, California, analyzed auto-related municipal expenditures for that city of 132,000, slightly larger than Boise. He found that auto-related costs to local government totaled nearly $16 million in 1985, of which drivers paid directly for only about one-quarter. If auto-related municipal expenditures in the Pacific Northwest are comparable, then the municipal services subsidy in the region could run well over a billion dollars annually.[67]

WITH DRIVERS PAYING SO LITTLE FOR THE SERVICES THEY REQUIRE, OTHERS MUST PAY MORE.

By assuming many of the costs of driving, government subsidies exacerbate auto dependency, sprawl, and pollution. Artificially low prices encourage people to drive; low-density suburbs, where public transit is seldom cost effective, tend to expand. Excessive auto traffic discourages walking or bicycling, and increasing numbers of cars create pressure to widen roads and re-engineer them for faster traffic flow, further discouraging walking and biking. The net effect of subsidizing driving is that fewer and fewer people use modes of transport that require less imported petroleum, consume less open space, and pollute the atmosphere less.

Sprawl

Over the last forty years, as low-cost automotive travel became widely available, suburbs have expanded greatly. Today more northwesterners live in suburbs than in cities, towns, or rural areas; new developments sprawl across parts of the Pacific Northwest landscape that until recently were covered by forest and farm land.[68]

Suburban sprawl has made the automobile virtually indispensable for many people, increasing the costs the public must pay for the automobile. Sprawl is characterized by both low-density land use and zoning codes that mandate strict segregation of residential and commercial land uses. The result: the large distances that separate people's homes from shops, services, and work sites can conveniently be bridged only by driving.

Providing road, water, storm drainage, sewer, and school services to sprawling developments is much more costly than providing these services to more compact developments. Though municipalities collect "impact fees" on new construction to recover the costs of public services, these fees are usually assessed equally on all developments, even though sprawl can cost twice as much. (A 1989 study by the Urban Land Institute found that providing roads, sewer lines, and other public services to new housing developments costs $23,000 per house in compact neighborhoods but as much as $48,000 in low-density developments.) As a result, people who choose to live near town centers where public service costs are lower typically subsidize those who move to the suburbs.[69]

Various programs in the U.S. subsidize sprawl by assuming the costs of building in risky areas. The National Flood Insurance Program offers subsidized insurance that encourages home construction on floodplains and near exposed coastlines, areas that private firms often will not insure. The U.S. Forest Service safeguards, at great expense, remote ranches and vacation homes—providing a hugely expensive form of fire insurance at no charge. The agency effectively has a standing blank check to spend whatever it takes to fight fires, many of which can be extinguished only by rain or snow. In summer 1994, the Forest Service spent $35 million to protect a few ranches from burning in Idaho's Payette National Forest. Aggressive fire suppression policies in effect subsidize sprawl into woodlands, in turn making ecologically sound management of fire-dependent forests increasingly difficult.[70]

Undoing Subsidies

Before the helicopter came, things were different. On the east side of the mountains, the Cheslatta Band lived on the abundant salmon, game, and wild plants of the Nechako River basin. To the west, the Haisla ("the people who live at the river mouth") depended on the living wealth of the lower Kitimat River, one of the few places on the rugged British Columbia coast with relatively flat land, and a correspondingly rich estuary.

On April 3, 1952, officials of the Canada Department of Indian Affairs and the Aluminum Company of Canada (now Alcan) stepped out of a helicopter and told the Cheslatta that they would have to move immediately. The province had given Alcan the rights to all the water of the Nechako River—an unprecedented incentive to build the world's largest aluminum smelter in a remote rain forest. The Cheslatta's lands, 80,000 acres (32,000 hectares) of forest, would soon be flooded. Informed a few weeks before being forced from their land, the Cheslatta would later receive what the Vancouver Sun called a "contemptible pittance" in compensation.

For four years, while the 300-mile (450-kilometer) Nechako reservoir filled behind Alcan's massive rock dam, almost no water left the upper Nechako River, and its chinook salmon were nearly eliminated. Since then, 30 to 70 percent of the river's flow has been diverted each year through massive tunnels under the Coast Range toward the Pacific, where it powers Alcan's smelter. Pulses of water, flushed seasonally down a spillway into the Cheslatta River, have carried 40 million cubic meters of plants, rocks, and soil downstream into Cheslatta Lake and carved a canyon 25 miles long by 80 feet deep (40 kilometers by 25 meters).

The smelter itself sits on landfilled former mudflats, once a rich tidal environment for birds, fish, and shellfish. During the smelter's construction, 9,000 cubic meters of mud were dredged daily from the estuary to create a deep-water port. The dredging then, and for the past 40 years, has made a fine port for ships carrying aluminum across the Pacific. Its effects on the estuary have not been documented.

In 1988, Alcan announced that it would begin a second phase of its project, to divert most of what remained of the Nechako River to its powerhouse. The Kemano Completion Project, as this phase is known, would reduce the flow of the Nechako to 13 percent of its original levels. The federal government exempted the project from Canada's environmental assessment act—an unprecedented move for such a large project. Legal battles held up construction for years.

The Nechako is the third-largest tributary of the Fraser River, British Columbia's largest river and the world's greatest salmon producer. Twenty percent of the Fraser's sockeye salmon—a million or more fish—swim up the lower Nechako to spawn in high mountain lakes. The dramatically reduced flows would jeopardize their epic migration and possibly the migration of salmon from all over the B.C. interior past the Hell's Gate fish ladders on the main stem of the Fraser, a few hundred miles downstream.

By the 1990s, the Cheslatta and other native bands, environmentalists, and even government fisheries scientists had organized to prevent the further dewatering of the Nechako. Responding to their complaints *and to shifting public opinion polls, the B.C. government canceled the Kemano Completion Project in early 1995. The provincial and federal governments and Alcan now debate who should pay Alcan, and how much, in compensation for the fraction of the river given to it in 1952 and effectively taken back in 1995. Alcan continues to remove, and pay little for, 70 percent of the Nechako's flow. The Cheslatta continue to press for the return of their land. They also demand that more water be left in the Nechako, to ensure that the river never stops flashing red and silver with millions of salmon.[71]*

Though many of the grants of land, water, resources, and cash described in this report have had disastrous effects on native peoples, natural systems, and government finances, it would be unfair to judge yesterday's actions by today's standards. It does not follow, however, that today's actions must be guided by yesterday's standards. Yet public policy toward land, energy, transportation, water, and other sectors of major environmental importance fits precisely this pattern. Laws from another century, such as the U.S. General Mining Law of 1872, continue to determine the shape of public policy and natural landscapes. Other subsidies—such as Alcan's Kemano deal—are more recent but arose when environmental concerns were few and economic theory directed governments to prime the economic engine with deficit spending and gifts to key industries.

The Northwest economy stands out from most of North America by its heavily subsidized sectors: electricity, irrigation, and various commodities drawn from public lands. But today, one of the main drivers of the Northwest economy is the "subsidy" from nature itself: the high quality of life made possible by a natural endowment less degraded than in other parts of the industrialized world. The Northwest's natural amenities provide what economists Ed Whitelaw and Ernie Niemi call a "second paycheck." Nature in the Northwest draws and retains people who work in footloose high-tech firms and in the service sector, whose growth is the main reason economies in the Northwest have been growing faster than those outside the region.[72]

Free-market economists generally regard subsidies as a drag on the economy as a whole, whether or not they serve a valid social purpose: they worsen tax burdens and distort the price signals that serve to allocate resources. But the subsidies described in this report do more than that. They waste billions of dollars, and they waste the one thing that dollars cannot buy—life, both our own and that of the ecological community that undergirds our economy. Publicly owned forests are overcut; our mountains leached with cyanide; our air polluted; and our rivers dammed, dredged, and drained—all at our expense. Old ways of doing public business immediately threaten the Northwest's "second paycheck" and the vitality of its changing economy. In the long term, they endanger the viability of the natural systems upon which all economic activity depends. Billions of dollars in tax payments could be saved each year if these subsidies were removed. Untold billions in environmental damage, and expenditures to repair that damage, could also be avoided.[73]

Despite the powerful arguments against them, subsidies to environmentally harmful activities have proved exceptionally hard to undo. Why are these costly and destructive handouts themselves nearly indestructible? Perhaps because subsidies generally redistribute wealth to a small number of beneficiaries from a large number of unknowing or unwilling contributors—whether taxpayers or Native Americans, like the Cheslatta. The few industries or individuals who receive most of the benefits lobby energetically to defend their handouts; the dispersed or disempowered contributors seldom do.

Governments often seek to curb the impacts of antienvironmental subsidies, without upsetting those who benefit, by proposing even more subsidies. BPA, for example, has a "water wise" program to subsidize efficiency improvements on irrigated farmland as a means of conserving the electricity used to pump water. Yet the agency's 20 percent discount on electricity sold to irrigators, which discourages conservation, remains. In a 1994 report on disincentives to sustainable economic practices, the Canadian federal government recommended a variety of new subsidies for recycling and public transit but almost entirely refrained from criticizing or suggesting reductions in existing antienvironmental subsidies.[74]

Attempts to level the playing field by propping up less-subsidized activities may achieve some environmental gains. But the practice cannot go on, as fiscal crises in Ottawa, Washington, D.C., and throughout the Northwest attest. And the more the playing field is propped up, the more the players as a whole lose sight of the ground beneath them—the natural systems at the base of the economy.

Defenders of below-cost electricity or timber or subsidized mortgages argue that cutting subsidies would have wrenching effects on the economy and on the way people live. Yet despite professed concerns for their workers, many industries that defend subsidies employ few people and for decades have been reducing employment through mechanization. It is not coincidental that these capital-intensive industries have disproportionate environmental impacts: they use energy, chemicals, raw materials, and machinery in large amounts and rely relatively little on human labor.

Reducing subsidies would have major economic impacts, good for some people and bad for others. Reductions should be phased in to avoid undue disruption, and their distributive effects carefully evaluated. Tremendous savings in supports for housing and agriculture, for example, could be realized if subsidies in these sectors were directed to people who actually require assistance to obtain housing or produce food, rather than to wealthy homeowners and large agricultural businesses. Welfare applicants must pass a needs test; governments could enact similar provisions for natural resource subsidies.

In early 1995, state, provincial, and national governments in North America were pursuing major cuts in spending. Canadian Finance Minister Paul Martin unveiled his government's 1995-96 budget in February, proposing cuts for a wide range of programs, including social programs and some antienvironment subsidies. Unless budget cuts are targeted toward those programs that benefit the wealthiest class, they will have regressive social impacts: a dollar lost by a poor person does more harm than a dollar lost by a rich person. Budget cuts passed by the Appropriations Committee of the U.S. House of Representatives in March are strongly regressive, sparing antienvironment "corporate welfare" programs and cutting deeply into programs for the poor. Two-thirds of the proposed cuts come from programs that assist low-income people, even though these programs account for only 12 percent of the U.S. government's discretionary spending (funding that can legally be cut).[75]

OLD WAYS OF DOING PUBLIC BUSINESS ENDANGER THE NATURAL SYSTEMS UPON WHICH ALL ECONOMIC ACTIVITY DEPENDS.

Such budget-cutting measures have been accompanied by calls for more-drastic reductions in the role of government, including the privatization of public lands and quasi-public agencies like the Bonneville Power Administration. Governments should not abdicate their responsibility to provide a social safety net and to curb the environmental excesses of the market economy. Though government often fares poorly in pursuing public goals, it at least *has* public goals; experience has repeatedly proved wrong those who assumed that private firms would pursue or even act neutrally toward such goals. Subsidized logging on public lands has depleted old-growth forests throughout the Northwest, but it is worth noting that practically all the old growth left remains on public lands. Private landowners cleared theirs long ago.

Though some natural resource extraction would halt if it were no longer subsidized, reducing antienvironment subsidies will not by itself make our economy environmentally sound. Large-scale logging of southeast Alaskan rain forest, for example, simply would not occur if the U.S. government did not pay for it. But reduced subsidies will not always lead to reduced environmental impacts. Even if BLM charges full market rates for the privilege of grazing public land, destructive grazing will probably continue unless the agency establishes stricter land management guidelines.

A variety of other reforms, some costly, must be pursued in tandem with money-saving reforms such as subsidy reductions, if the environment is to benefit. At the very least, subsidies mask the costliness of government's current way of managing the environment; reducing subsidies will at the least help pay for other environmental reforms. Power and water subsidies to irrigators cost the average BPA customer $2 to $4 per month, roughly twice the amount needed to modify dams on the Columbia and Snake Rivers to improve migration conditions for salmon. If funded solely by BPA, structural modifications of the four lower Snake River dams necessary to allow faster and safer downstream passage for endangered salmon stocks would cost the average BPA customer $0.75 to 1.50 per month.[76]

Overcoming government inertia and the lobbying power of industry is not easy. But if enough people feel that money and natural endowments are too precious to waste, subsidies *can* be overcome, as the cancellation of the Kemano Completion Project shows. The Fraser River, in the words of B.C. Premier Mike Harcourt, is the "soul of British Columbia." As the Northwest's (and the world's) largest producer of salmon, the river is of tremendous importance to people outside B.C. as well.[77]

It would have been much easier, of course, had the B.C. government rejected the Completion Project in the first place, instead of aggressively pursuing it for years. Taxpayers may receive little in direct savings because Alcan is seeking compensation for the sudden withdrawal of its promised subsidy. And even as it seeks payment from the provincial government, the company continues to pay next to nothing for 70 percent of the Nechako's flow and benefits from other governmental favors. In 1993, as Alcan's annual report noted, the company owed Can$888 million in deferred taxes.[78]

Though the intertwined fates of the Nechako River and Alcan's subsidies are far from sealed, the B.C. government's decision to at least avoid making further mistakes with the public's money and natural capital is encouraging. Current political climates in both Canada and the U.S. bode poorly for the environment, but the possibility that politicians of all party stripes can embrace one of the most important steps toward an environmentally sound economy offers a sign of hope. As Camp Creek and the Cheslatta River show, we can no longer afford to let subsidies rip canyons in our economies or our landscapes.

IN 1993, ALCAN OWED NEARLY CAN$900 MILLION IN DEFERRED TAXES.

NOTES

1. All quotations and history of Camp Creek from Charles F.Wilkinson, *Crossing the Next Meridian: Land, Water, and the Future of the West* (Washington, D.C.: Island Press, 1992); current conditions of Camp Creek also based on Bill Marlett, Oregon Natural Desert Association, Bend, Ore., private communication, Feb. 28, 1995.
2. Wilkinson, op. cit. note 1.
3. Grazing rates on private land in Oregon for 1994 averaged $9.00 per animal-unit-month; BLM rates in 1994 were $1.98 per AUM; see Table 9 and endnote 42.
4. U.S. House Committee on Natural Resources, Subcommittee on Oversight and Investigations, *Taking from the Taxpayer: Public Subsidies for Natural Resource Development* (Washington, D.C.: U.S. Government Printing Office, 1994).
5. Wilkinson, op. cit. note 1.
6. Early history described in Wilkinson, op. cit. note 1; U.S. National Forest harvest from Paul Hirt, "Timber Dreams…," *Inner Voice,* May–June 1994; B.C. harvest from O. R. Travers, "Forest Policy: Rhetoric and Reality," in Ken Drushka et al., eds., *Touch Wood: BC Forests at the Crossroads* (Madeira Park, B.C.: Harbour Publishing, 1993).
7. Table 1 based on Statistics Canada, *Canadian Yearbook 1994* (Ottawa: 1994); B.C. Ministry of Environment, Lands, and Parks and Environment Canada, *State of the Environment Report for British Columbia* (Victoria and NorthVancouver: 1993); Philip L. Jackson and A. Jon Kimerling, eds., *Atlas of the Pacific Northwest,* 8th ed. (Corvallis: Oregon State Univ. Press, 1993); U.S. Department of Commerce, Bureau of the Census, *County and City Data Book, 1994* (Washington, D.C.: 1994); U.S. Department of Agriculture (USDA), Forest Service, *Land Area of the National Forest System* (Washington, D.C.: 1992); Rick Griffen, USDA Forest Service, Juneau, private communication, June 8, 1994; Randy Hagenstein, Pacific GIS, Anchorage, private communication, Mar. 10, 1995.
8. Travers, op. cit. note 6; $2 billion figure based on Michael Mascall, "Public Investment by Governments in the BC Forest Industry 1991–92," Michael Mascall & Associates, Quathiaski Cove, B.C., Mar. 1994. (In contrast to Mascall, figure here does not include unemployment payments to timber workers as an investment in the forest industry.)
9. Travers, op. cit. note 6.
10. Travers, op. cit. note 6; Mascall, op cit. note 8.
11. U.S. House Committee on Natural Resources, op. cit. note 4; Carolyn Alkire, *Financial Losses from Logging on National Forests, FY 1993,* The Wilderness Society, Washington D.C., Nov. 1994.
12. U.S. House Committee on Natural Resources, op. cit. note 4.

13. Table 2 based on Alkire, op. cit. note 11; U.S. Department of Agriculture, Forest Service, *Timber Sale Program Annual Report, Fiscal Year 1993* (Washington, D.C.: 1994).

14. U.S. House Committee on Natural Resources, op. cit. note 4; BLM acreage from Claire A. Puchy and David B. Marshall, *Oregon Wildlife Diversity Plan* (Portland: Oregon Department of Fish and Wildlife, 1993).

15. U.S. House Committee on Natural Resources, op. cit. note 4.

16. U.S. House Committee on Natural Resources, op. cit. note 4; Plum Creek acreage and grizzly bear habitat from Rocky Barker, *Saving All the Parts: Reconciling Economics and the Endangered Species Act* (Washington, D.C.: Island Press, 1993).

17. Mascall, op. cit. note 8.

18. Gordon Gregory, "Big Timber Keeps More of Its Green," *Grants Pass (Ore.) Daily Courier,* June 30, 1994; Josephine County from Gordon Gregory, "Forest Assessments Look Too Low," *Grants Pass Daily Courier,* July 1, 1994; deficit from Gordon Gregory, "Tax Break: A Gift or a Show of Power?" *Grants Pass Daily Courier,* July 2, 1994.

19. Peter Dreier and John Atlas, "The Scandal of Mansion Subsidies," *Dissent,* winter 1992; Jeanne W. Wolfe, "Canada's Liveable Cities," *Social Policy,* summer 1992.

20. Jason DeParle, "Report to Clinton Sees Vast Extent of Homelessness," *New York Times,* Feb. 17, 1994; construction sector wood consumption from Alan Thein Durning, *Saving the Forests: What Will It Take?* (Washington, D.C.: Worldwatch Institute, December 1993); Dreier and Atlas, op. cit. note 19.

21. Wilkinson, op. cit. note 1; U.S. House Committee on Natural Resources, op. cit. note 4.

22. Thomas J. Hilliard et al., *Golden Patents, Empty Pockets* (Washington, D.C.: Mineral Policy Center, 1994); U.S. House Committee on Natural Resources, op. cit. note 4.

23. Hilliard et al., op cit. note 22.

24. Hilliard et al., op cit. note 22; U.S. House Committee on Natural Resources, op. cit. note 4; Wilkinson, op. cit. note 1.

25. Mineral production from Wilma Hannoca, Land Management and Policy Branch, B.C. Ministry of Energy, Mines, and Petroleum Resources, Victoria, private communication, Feb. 13, 1995, and from U.S. Department of the Interior, Bureau of Mines, *Mineral Industry Surveys 1993* (Washington, D.C.: 1994); B.C. Ministry of Corporate and Financial Relations, *1994 Financial and Economic Review* (Victoria: 1994); Alan Young, Environmental Mining Council of British Columbia, Victoria, B.C., private communication, Jan. 17, 1995; Ken Sumanik, Mining Association of B.C., Vancouver, private communication, Jan. 31, 1995.

26. U.S. House Committee on Natural Resources, op. cit. note 4.

27. U.S. House Committee on Natural Resources, op. cit. note 4; reclamation bonds from B.C. Ministry of Energy, Mines, and Petroleum (EMP), *Mine Reclamation Security Policy in British Columbia* (Vancouver: 1995), and John

Errington, EMP, Mineral Resources Division, Victoria, private communication, Feb. 22, 1995; Table 4 based on U.S. Environmental Protection Agency, Office of Solid Waste, *Mining Sites on the NPL* (Washington, D.C.: 1994); Western Governors' Association, *Inactive and Abandoned Noncoal Mines: A Scoping Study* (Denver, Colo.: Aug. 1991).

28. John E. Young, *Mining the Earth* (Washington, D.C.: Worldwatch Institute, July 1992).

29. Young, op. cit. note 28; John E. Young, "For the Love of Gold," *WorldWatch,* May–June 1993; Bureau of Mines research from U.S. House Committee on Natural Resources, op. cit. note 4; Idaho cyanide examples from Hilliard et al., op. cit. note 22.

30. John C. Ryan, "Northwest Employment Depends Less on Timber and Mining," *NEW Indicators* series, Northwest Environment Watch, Seattle, Nov. 1994; Ickes quote from Hilliard et al., op. cit. note 22.

31. U.S. House Committee on Natural Resources, op. cit. note 4.

32. Jackson and Kimerling, eds., op. cit. note 7. Table 5 based on U.S. Department of Commerce, Bureau of the Census, *1992 Census of Agriculture* (Washington, D.C.: 1994); B.C. Ministry of Agriculture, Fisheries, and Food, *Annual Statistics 1992* (Victoria: 1994); U.S. Department of Agriculture, Economic Research Service, *Agricultural Irrigation and Water Use,* Agricultural Information Bulletin No. 638 (Washington, D.C.: 1992); Statistics Canada, *Human Activity and the Environment, 1994* (Ottawa: 1994).

33. Wilkinson, op. cit. note 1.

34. Wilkinson, op. cit. note 1.

35. U.S. House Committee on Natural Resources, op. cit. note 4; Wilkinson, op. cit. note 1.

36. Columbia Basin Institute, "Water Conservation for Instream Recapture on the Bureau of Reclamation's Columbia Basin Project: Opportunities and Obstacles," testimony submitted to U.S. House Committee on Natural Resources, Subcommittee on Oversight and Investigations, Washington, D.C., July 19, 1994; BPA irrigator discounts from U.S. House Committee on Natural Resources, *BPA at a Crossroads* (Washington, D.C.: 1994); John Carros, B.C. Hydro, Rates and Prices Department, Burnaby, B.C., private communication, Feb. 8, 1995. Table 6 based on U.S. House Committee on Natural Resources, *BPA at a Crossroads;* Columbia Basin Institute, testimony; Norman K. Whittlesey et al., "Water Project Subsidies: How They Develop and Grow," *Illahee* 11, spring 1995.

37. Tim Palmer, *The Snake River: Window to the West* (Washington, D.C.: Island Press, 1991); hydropower values based on BPA's 1993 priority firm preference rate and its marginal cost of energy purchases, from William Bean and Rick Gove (Columbia Basin Institute), "BPA's Irrigated Agriculture Policy: Water Conservation and Energy Pricing," testimony to the U.S. House Committee on Natural Resources, BPA Task Force, Nov. 1, 1993.

38. Palmer, op. cit note 37.

39. U.S. House Committee on Natural Resources, op. cit. note 4; wheat exports from Elizabeth Losos et al., *Taxpayers' Double Burden: Federal Resource Subsidies and Endangered Species* (Washington, D.C.: The Wilderness Society, 1993); Corps costs from Karen Miller, U.S. Army Corps of Engineers, Finance Office, Portland, Ore., private communication, Mar. 6, 1995. "Columbia River Deepening Studied," *Environmental News Briefing,* Sept. 19, 1994.

40. Michael Pitt and Tracey D. Hooper, "Threats to Biodiversity of Grasslands in British Columbia," in Lee E. Harding and Emily McCullum, eds., *Biodiversity in British Columbia: Our Changing Environment* (Vancouver: Canadian Wildlife Service, 1994). Table 7 based on U.S. Department of Commerce, op. cit. note 32; U.S. Department of the Interior, Bureau of Land Management (BLM), *Public Land Statistics 1992* (Washington, D.C.: 1993); B.C. Ministry of Agriculture, op. cit. note 32; Bill Volk, BLM Montana State Office, Billings, private communication, Jan. 9, 1995; Jim Morrison, BLM California State Office, Sacramento, private communications, Jan. 9, 1995 and Mar. 2, 1995; Miriam Walters, Washington State Department of Natural Resources, Resources Planning Division, Olympia, private communication, Dec. 28, 1994; Jeff Croft, Oregon Division of State Lands, Portland, private communication, Dec. 27, 1994; Don Hobbs, Idaho State Lands Department, Boise, private communication, Dec. 27, 1994; Jeff Hagener, Montana Department of State Lands, Helena, private communication, Dec. 23, 1994.

41. U.S. House Committe on Natural Resources, op. cit. note 4; "Babbitt Backs off Grazing Fees," *Seattle Times,* Dec. 22, 1994. Table 8 based on BLM, op. cit. note 40; B.C. Ministry of Forests, *Annual Report 92–93* (Victoria: 1993); Earl Jensen, B.C. Ministry of Forests, Range Branch, Victoria, private communication, Jan. 3, 1995; Volk, note 40; Morrison, note 40.

42. Table 9 based on U.S. Department of Agriculture, National Agricultural Statistics Service, *Agricultural Prices December 1994* (Washington, D.C.: 1994); Jensen, note 41; Linda Martinez, California State Lands Department, Sacramento, private communication, Jan. 3, 1995; Walters, note 40; Croft, note 40; Hobbs, note 40; Hagener, note 40.

43. U.S. House Committee on Natural Resources, op. cit. note 4; Whittlesey et al., op. cit. note 36.

44. Farm program costs from U.S. Department of Commerce, op. cit. note 32, and from B.C. Ministry of Agriculture, op. cit. note 32; environmental impact from Paul Faeth et al., *Paying the Farm Bill: U.S. Agricultural Policy and the Transition to Sustainable Agriculture* (Washington, D.C.: World Resources Institute, 1991).

45. U.S. Department of Energy, Energy Information Administration (EIA), *State Energy Data Report 1991* (Washington, D.C.: 1993); EIA, *Electric Power Annual 1992* (Washington, D.C.: 1994).

46. U.S. House Committee on Natural Resources, op. cit. note 36. Table 10:

Prices and total consumption based on Statistics Canada, *Electric Power Statistics* (Ottawa: 1994); EIA, *Electric Power Annual,* op. cit. note 45; Montana Environmental Quality Council, *Energy Policy Study* (Helena: 1993); and Cheryl Hansen, Montana Power Company, Butte, private communication, Feb. 3, 1995. Population data from U.S. and Canadian censuses.

47. U.S. House Committee on Natural Resources, op. cit. note 36; dam numbers from Timothy Egan, "A G.O.P. Attack Hits a Bit Too Close to Home," *New York Times,* Mar. 3, 1995.

48. U.S. Department of Energy, Energy Information Administration, *Federal Energy Subsidies: Direct and Indirect Interventions in Energy Markets* (Washington, D.C.: 1992).

49. U.S. Department of Energy, op. cit. note 48; nuclear subsidies from Douglas Koplow, *Federal Energy Subsidies: Energy, Environmental, and Fiscal Impacts* (Lexington, Mass.: Alliance to Save Energy, 1993); Eric Pryne, "Regional Icons May Face Budget Ax," *Seattle Times,* Nov. 10, 1994.

50. *Plugging People into Power: An Energy Participation Handbook* (Seattle Northwest Conservation Act Coalition, 1993); B.C. Hydro, *Annual Report 1994* (Vancouver: 1994); Timo Macinen, B.C. Hydro, Load Forecasting Dept., private communication, Mar. 8, 1995.

51. Subsidies over past decade from U.S. House Committee on Natural Resources, op. cit. note 4, and U.S. House Committee on Natural Resources, op. cit. note 36; $2 per month comparison from the Save Our Wild Salmon Coalition, *Wild Salmon Forever: A Citizens' Strategy to Restore Northwest Salmon and Watersheds* (Seattle: 1995).

52. Jennifer S. Gitlitz, *The Relationship between Primary Aluminum Production and the Damming of World Rivers* (Berkeley, Calif.: International Rivers Network, 1993).

53. BPA electricity from Douglas Koplow, "Federal Energy Subsidies and Recycling," *Resource Recycling,* Nov. 1994; Oregon Department of Energy, "Draft Report on Reducing Oregon's Greenhouse Gas Emissions," Salem, 1994.

54. BPA smelters (eight in Washington and one in Montana) produce 39 percent of U.S. primary aluminum, according to Koplow, op. cit. note 53. Table 11 based on International Primary Aluminum Institute, *Electric Power Utilization: Annual Report for 1993* (London: 1994); Washington figure based on Bonneville Power Administration, *Generation and Sales Statistics, 1993* (Portland, Ore.: 1994), and Pat Plunkert, U.S. Bureau of Mines, Washington, D.C., private communication, Feb. 3, 1995; B.C. figure based on Karen Kirby, B.C. Stats, Victoria, private communication, Feb. 15, 1995.

55. Gitlitz, op. cit. note 52.

56. Losos, op. cit. note 39.

57. Salmon decline based on Northwest Power Planning Council, *Strategy for Salmon,* vol. 1 (Portland: 1992), and on Burnie Bohn, Oregon Department of Fish and Wildlife, Portland, private communication, Aug. 10, 1994; John C. Ryan, *State of the Northwest* (Seattle: Northwest Environment Watch, 1994).

58. Ray M. Northam, "Transportation," in Jackson and Kimerling, eds., op. cit. note 7; B.C. Round Table on the Economy and the Environment, *State of Sustainability* (Victoria: Crown Publications, 1994).

59. Road mileage in Federal Highway Administration (FHA), *Highway Statistics 1993* (Washington, D.C.: 1994).

60. Table 12 based on FHA, op. cit. note 59; B.C. Ministry of Finance and Corporate Relations, *British Columbia Financial and Economic Review,* 54th ed. (Victoria: 1994); B.C. Ministry of Transportation and Highways, *Annual Report 1992–93* (Victoria: 1993); B.C. Ministry of Municipal Affairs, *Municipal Statistics, 1992* (Victoria: 1993); Dan Carlson, B.C. Ministry of Municipal Affairs, Victoria, private communication, Feb. 27, 1995.

61. Gas prices and taxes from International Energy Agency, *Energy Prices and Taxes: Second Quarter 1993* (Paris: Organisation for Economic Co-operation and Development, 1993); roadwork subsidies from FHA, op. cit. note 59; gas tax increase based on 5.2 billion gallons of motor fuel consumed annually in Idaho, Oregon, and Washington in 1993, from Federal Highway Administration, op. cit. note 59, and 5.1 million liters consumed in British Columbia, from Teresa Taaffe, B.C. Ministry of Finance and Corporate Relations, Victoria, private communication, Feb., 1995.

62. Todd Litman, *Transportation Cost Analysis: Techniques, Estimates, and Implications* (Victoria: Transport Policy Institute, 1995).

63. King County Department of Metropolitan Services, Transit Department, Research and Market Strategy Division, *1994 Rider/Non-Rider Survey* (draft report) (Seattle: 1995); Donald C. Shoup, *Cashing Out Employer-Paid Parking* (Washington, D.C.: U.S. Department of Transportation, Federal Transit Administration, Office of Technical Assistance and Safety, 1992); *Transport 2021: The Cost of Transporting People in the British Columbia Lower Mainland,* Tech. Rep. 11 (Vancouver: Greater Vancouver Regional District and the Province of British Columbia, 1993.)

64. Shoup, op. cit. note 63.

65. Todd Litman, transportation analyst, Victoria, private communication, Mar. 1, 1995.

66. Shoup, op. cit. note 63.

67. Stanley I. Hart and Alvin L. Spivak, *Automobile Dependence and Denial: The Elephant in the Bedroom* (Pasadena: New Paradigm Books, 1993); James J. MacKenzie et al., *The Going Rate: What It Really Costs to Drive* (Washington, D.C.: World Resources Institute, 1992).

68. Alan Thein Durning, "Vehicles Outnumber Drivers in the Northwest," *NEW Indicators* series, Northwest Environment Watch, Seattle, Jan. 11, 1995.

69. Costs, in 1987 U.S. dollars, are from James E. Frank, *The Costs of Alternative Development Patterns: A Review of the Literature* (Washington, D.C.: Urban Land Institute: 1989); Kevin Kasowski, "The Costs of Sprawl, Revisited," *Developments* (newsletter of the National Growth Management Leadership Project, Portland, Ore.), Sept. 1992.

70. Growth Management Planning and Research Clearinghouse, University of Washington, *A Literature Review of Community Impacts and Costs of Urban Sprawl* (Washington, D.C.: National Trust for Historic Preservation, 1993); Michael Paterniti, "The Great Western Fire Sale," *New York Times,* Jan. 7, 1995.

71. Kemano history from Gitlitz, op. cit. note 52, Dirk Beck, "The Kemano Deal: Scientists, Salmon Sacrificed," *The Watershed* (newsletter of the Carrier-Sekani Tribal Council, Burns Lake, B.C.), Nov. 1993, and Dana Wagg, "The Kemano Projects: The Main Events," *The Watershed,* Nov. 1993; "contemptible pittance" from Stephen Hume, "Possible Breach of Duty Identified in Kemano Brief," *Vancouver Sun,* Jan. 20, 1995; Fraser River sockeye numbers from T. G. Northcote and D.Y. Atagi, "Pacific Salmon Abundance Trends in the Fraser River Watershed Compared with Other British Columbia Systems," paper presented at "Pacific Salmon and Their Ecosystems: Status and Future Options," a conference held in Seattle, Jan. 10–12, 1994; greatest salmon producer from B.C. Ministry of Environment, Lands, and Parks and Environment Canada, op. cit. note 7.

72. The phrase "second paycheck" appears in W. Ed Whitelaw and Ernest G. Niemi, "Money: The Greening of the Economy," *Old Oregon,* spring 1989; Ryan, op. cit. note 30.

73. See T. M. Power, *Extraction and the Environment: The Economic Battle to Control Our Natural Landscapes* (Washington, D.C.: Island Press, forthcoming).

74. U.S. House Committee on Natural Resources, op. cit. note 36; Canada Department of Finance and Environment Canada, *Economic Instruments and Disincentives to Sound Environmental Practices* (Ottawa: 1994).

75. Paul Martin, Finance Minister, budget speech to the House of Commons, Ottawa, Feb. 27, 1995; Center on Budget and Policy Priorities, "House Rescissions Would Hit Programs for the Poor," Washington, D.C., Mar. 7, 1995.

76. Save Our Wild Salmon Coalition, op. cit. note 51.

77. Harcourt quoted by Keith Baldrey, "Rough Water Looms for Kemano Project," *Vancouver Sun,* Jan. 12, 1995; Northcote and Atagi, op. cit. note 71.

78. Deferred taxes from Ross Howard, "B.C. Liable for Dam Compensation, Ottawa says," *(Toronto) Globe and Mail,* Jan. 25, 1995.

John C. Ryan *is research director at Northwest Environment Watch and author of* State of the Northwest *(Seattle: 1994). He has worked for local nonprofit groups in Indonesia and for Worldwatch Institute, where he wrote* Life Support: Conserving Biological Diversity *(Washington, D.C.: 1992). Ryan holds degrees in history from Stanford University and environmental history from Yale University.*

Rhys Roth *is director of the Atmosphere Alliance in Olympia and author of* Municipal Strategies to Increase Pedestrian Travel *(Olympia: Washington State Energy Office, 1994). He has a master's degree in environmental studies from Evergreen State College.*
